I0142584

A MILLIONAIRE OF LOVE

A few years ago Andrew Carnegie, by his generous gifts, made University education in Scotland possible to the many. Dr. Horton, a warm friend of Adult Schools, referring to it, said that the world needed, just as badly, millionaires of another kind, MILLIONAIRES OF LOVE. Such an one was Charles Hess, the possessor of a wealth of affection, freely bestowed on all who were in need.

CHARLES HESS.

A Millionaire of Love

THE LIFE STORY OF
CHARLES HESS
TOLD BY HIMSELF

Foreword by
J. ALLEN BAKER, M.P.

LONDON
HEADLEY BROTHERS
BISHOPSGATE STREET WITHOUT E.C.

FOREWORD.

———

CHARLES HESS, whose life of usefulness has been cut short at so early an age, was endowed with a nature of rare qualities. Though physically such a powerful man, he was as tender as a woman, and one could not fail to be impressed by the childlike simplicity of his faith in and love for his Lord. He had the imagination of a poet and the gift of an artist in presenting his thoughts in a clear and picturesque way. He possessed a large and sympathetic heart for the sinful and suffering, and had a simple and effective way of winning their confidence and influencing their lives. His own experience and the great change from his old life of sin and dissipation to an exemplary Christian walk and conversation, were so striking and wonderful to himself as to be a constant theme for private conversation or public discourse, and the change was so manifest and real that his daily life became an evidence of the power of the gospel of Christ, and the teaching received in the Adult School to change the lives of the most careless and sinful.

Having himself tasted the joy of forgiveness and of Christian fellowship with his brethren, his great desire and delight was to tell of that which he himself had found so precious. He was ever ready to respond to the many calls for service that came to him for Adult School and other meetings, and his earnest and graphic addresses and appeals were always listened to with wrapt attention by large or small audiences. He felt that the Adult School had a first claim on his time, and this movement, whose rapid growth for some years he had helped to promote, will long miss his devoted labours and personal influence.

J. ALLEN BAKER.

April, 1909.

INTRODUCTION.

HAVING been asked to supply a few particulars of the circumstances that brought Charles Hess under the influence of the Adult School, I have laid aside reluctance to speak of what is in some sense a personal matter, knowing that it was but a link in the chain of the Providence of God that had watched over all the years of his wanderings, and brought his feet at length into the right path.

It was in 1892 that Charles Hess applied for an engineer's post advertised by the firm of R. & J. Beck, only to learn from the gatekeeper that he was too late, the place being already filled. But, following one of those intuitions that so often guided him in his actions, he made up his mind that that particular place was the berth for him, and that somehow he would secure it. Being penniless at the time, he borrowed a halfpenny, bought paper and envelope, and returning to the works sent in a written application, and found, as he fully expected, that the gatekeeper had been mistaken, for the place was still open, and he was engaged on the spot.

One of the first things, he said, that attracted his attention was the fact that his new employer did not swear, and he confessed that over and over again when things went wrong he would make some excuse to get within hearing, only to turn away with what he described as rage in his heart, because it seemed a continual rebuke to him.

Finding him an intelligent workman, my brother, W. Beck, employed him frequently in his private workshop, and it was on one of these occasions that I received suddenly, while gardening, a vivid impression, as clear as if the words had been spoken aloud, " Go and tell Hess of the Adult School."   I knew nothing of his home life or circumstances, nor that his wife was dying, and that he had fully determined when her faithful and devoted love was removed, to take his own life.   Finding on inquiry that he was not attending any place of worship, I merely told him of the Bunhill School, and advised him to inquire for J. Allen Baker, in whose class I felt sure he would feel at home. He was ever a man of action, and I believe it was the next morning that, to the surprise of his family, he rose at six o'clock, pressed carefully, and made his way to Bunhill, receiving so warm a welcome there that from that day forward he never missed attending the School if it was in any way possible for him to be present. Those who knew his sincerity can imagine his look and the tone of his voice, as some weeks later in reply to the query whether he had found his way to the Adult School, he replied, " I promised."

There are few, perhaps, who knew how intense and terrible was his struggle against long-standing habits, especially during the time of loneliness after his wife's death; but again and again help reached him in remarkable and unexpected ways. During one of the few lapses, he was employed on work that took him to Tottenham, a place where he had lived formerly, and turning into a familiar haunt had ordered something at the bar, when he was accosted by an old acquaintance with the words, " What has happened to you ? you look so different." They went straight home, and saying, " Yes, I *am* different," he delivered a temperance address in his own forcible style to the occupants of the bar, and leaving what he had ordered untasted, walked out, and never again yielded to the temptation. He afterwards tried to seek out this old companion, in the hope of helping him, for his power of sympathy, combined with the sensitiveness of his temperament, and the fineness of feeling that he possessed in no ordinary degree, gave him great tact and intuition in speaking to individuals, as well as in addressing large audiences.

There seemed years of increasing usefulness before him, but his work here was done, and there were only the weeks of intense suffering to be borne so bravely and patiently, for in his own characteristic way he said, " I should like to pull out, but I mustn't complain ; God has been so good to me."

GERTRUDE BECK.

CONTENTS.

CHAPTER I.

Early Memories.

"ONCE upon a time a boy played about the house, running by his mother's side, and as he was very little his mother tied him to the string of her apron. 'Now,' she said, 'when you stumble, you can pull yourself up by the apron string, and so you will not fall.' The boy did that, and all went well, and the mother sang at her work.

"By and bye the boy grew so tall that his head came above the window sill, and looking through the window he saw far away green trees waving, and a flowing river that flashed in the sun, and, rising above all, blue peaks of mountains. 'Oh, mother,' he said, 'untie the apron string and let me go.' But the mother said, 'Not yet, my child; only yesterday you stumbled and would have fallen but for the apron string. Wait a little until you are stronger.'

"So the boy waited, and all went as before, and the mother sang at her work; but one day

the boy found the door of the house standing
open, for it was spring, and he stood on the
threshold and looked across the valley, and saw
the green trees waving and the swift-flowing
river with the sun flashing on it, and the blue
mountains rising beyond ; this time he heard
the voice of the river calling, and it said ' Come ! '

" Then the boy started forward, and as he
started, the string of the apron broke. ' Oh ! how
weak my mother's apron string is ! ' cried the boy ;
and he ran out into the world with the broken
string hanging beside him.   The mother gathered
up the other end of the string and put it in her
bosom, and went about her work again ; but
she sang no more.

" The boy ran on and on, rejoicing in his freedom,
and in the fresh air and the morning sun ; he
crossed the valley and began to climb the foot-hills,
among which the river flowed swiftly among rocks
and cliffs.   Now it was easy climbing, and again
it was steep and craggy, but always he looked
upward at the blue peaks beyond, and always
the voice of the river was in his ears, saying,
' Come ! '

" By and bye he came to the brink of a precipice
over which the river dashed in a cataract, foaming
and flashing, and sending up clouds of silver spray.
The spray filled his eyes so that he did not see
his footing clearly ; he grew dizzy, stumbled
and fell ; but, as he fell, something about him
caught on a point of rock at the precipice edge,

and held him so that he hung dangling over the abyss, and when he put up his hand to see what held him he found it was the broken string of the apron, which still hung by his side. ' Oh! how strong my mother's apron string is!' said the boy, and he drew himself up by it, stood firmly on his feet, and went on climbing towards the blue peaks of the mountains."

This fable, from the pen of Laura E. Richards,* an American lady, describes the story of my life in a nutshell; the beautiful language she has chosen has filled me with the desire to write down what I have felt and seen in my wanderings.

I was born in the greatest city of the world, in 1852. Up to my seventh year all went well; I loved the sun, moon and stars, and often pulled myself up by my mother's apron string. Then my parents went abroad, my father being a civil engineer. I lost the language I speak now—picked up the German, listened to the voice of the swift-running Isar, and looked at the Alps beyond. So it happened, one spring morning, the doors and windows of this beautiful world stood wide open, and I ran away from home.

My mother clasped her hands to her bosom, went silent about her work, and sang no more.

I ran on, rejoicing in freedom, the sun and fresh air, the green fields dipping like the waves of the sea, the scenery ever changing, vineyards

* *The Golden Windows*, Laura E. Richards.   (Allenson.)

slanting up the hills. Passing through acres upon acres of fields,—some red, some white, some blue,—forbidding-looking castles in the distance, many a cottage near, and the river like a mass of molten silver ; on I went, through many a city, through dales and over hills,—sometimes easy climbing, sometimes steep and craggy,—but at the age of forty-three I could no longer see my footing clearly. I grew dizzy, stumbled and fell, was hanging over an abyss, and then the broken string of my mother's apron, —her prayers—caught round a rock, and I was pulled up out of the quagmire into which I was sinking in misery and despair, by the hand of a lady.

"Oh ! how strong my mother's apron string was."

Now I stand firmly on my feet, climbing towards the blue mountains, holding out a helping hand to whoever is in need.

Experience has taught me that though evil holds sway, to a very large extent, in this world, there is far more good than evil in it,—that God dwells in the humble cottage as well as in marble halls and palaces, in foreign countries as well as in England. I found good and bad wherever I went—most good. Hence these reminiscences.

CHAPTER II

The Sons of Vulcan.

A BEAUTIFUL custom prevailed in Bavaria, half the population being Protestant, the other half Catholic,—the King having married a Protestant Queen,—and the harmony among the people was perfect. Queen Maria I saw every Sunday as she went to the little Protestant Church. The King Maximillian I saw only once, and that was when he laid in his coffin. He was buried with all the pomp that priestcraft could invent; but the people wept, for they loved him.

I was at that time an apprentice,—all the shops were closed, and every man, woman and child went into mourning. I shall never forget this solemn procession marching through the streets, and the people bowing down with grief; innumerable maidens led the way, carrying plates of cut flowers, then the servants followed; the coffin was carried by generals, and the riderless horse, as if knowing its loss, came limping behind. Then, beneath a canopy carried by priests, came the Bishops with the perfume of myrrh and incense.

I heard the tolling of the bells, the fanfare of the trumpets and the shouting of the heralds: " The King is dead. Long live the King." I saw King Ludwig bowed down with grief, hat in hand, as if realising that in the midst of life he was in death, and that kings are not always the happiest of people.

Maybe through living among these large-hearted people my heart began to throb too. Maybe through going to school with the sons of artists, I became a lover of nature too. Maybe the clear sky, the crystal river, the blue mountains, the black forests, the birds and butterflies, helped to fill my heart with an ever-increasing desire for freedom— who can tell ?

I said " Good-bye " to the beautiful city of Munich nearly forty years ago, and have been a rolling stone ever since.

I went straight for Hamburg, the Eldorado of most of the mechanics in the Fatherland. It was astonishing the many friends I found while my money lasted, and how quickly they disappeared when my last penny was spent.

I was a pretty tall fellow, tried to appear like a man and spoke in a gruff voice ; but I was only a boy, and a silly boy at that.

I left Hamburg for Stettin, and walked across country, penniless, with a heavy knapsack on my back. I had plenty of time to think about my folly on the hard and stony road. Should I write to my mother ? No. I would sooner die in a ditch than let her know of my sorrow and plight. I looked with different eyes at the world now that I was hard up; I made many a promise to turn over a new leaf as soon as I could get work.

Stettin, a fortified town on the river Oder, bristled with barrels of herrings and soldiers when I arrived, but I wasn't wanted, so I went through a village called Grabo, and arrived at another called Bredo. The road passed right through a huge factory called the " Vulcan." On the right they turned out ships, and on the left they made locomotives; ten thousand hands were employed at that time.

A board hung up at the gate, saying " Fitters wanted," so I applied.

" Are you a good fitter ? " said the foreman.

" Yes!" said I, knowing well I was but a newly-fledged apprentice, with no experience at all.

However, I was engaged, and had to sign the rules. A hammer, half-a-dozen chisels and a file were served out to me from the stores, I was led to a bench in the wheel-trimmers' shop, and I was instructed to trim the spokes of a rough wheel. The noise was deafening. A cold shiver ran over me as I looked at the job hanging on a chain. Though I pulled myself together and tried to act the man, my blows were feeble, and the hammer often came down on my hand instead of the chisel. Moved through pity, some of the strong Pomeranians who worked by the side of me helped and explained, but it seemed all in vain, and when that day's work was over there was but little accomplished.

One of the men offered me food and lodging, another said I could have as much beer as I wanted, and that I could pay him for it on Saturday. Still another offered me money—at the rate of a half-penny in the shilling; I forgot all the promises I made on the road, and accepted from all.

Next day my head ached, and my hand bled more and more. When the foreman came his round I was fit to cry with shame.

" You don't seem to be much of a fitter," he said, " to get your hand in such a state."

" No," I whimpered. " I am a turner, but I thought I could do this work, and I wanted a job."

He picked up my tools and told me to come along. I thought I should get the sack, but he only handed me over to the other foreman and whispered something in his ear.

Going through many a shop full of wonderful machinery,—passing huge steam-hammers, bobbing up and down, making me tremble, sparks flying in all directions, steam hissing, taking my breath away,—we stepped into a shop with thousands of belts and wheels running in all directions. Axles, cranks, cylinders were being turned, bored, planed and machined: the groaning, hissing, squeaking and scratching were music to my ear, and I was filled with awe and admiration; I had never seen such a magnificent sight before.

" Look," said the foreman, " you shall have another chance since you make out you are not a fitter." So we mounted a platform of a twin surfacing lathe. "The work is already chucked for you, mind you don't act the goat ; the man has gone home ill and this job is wanted. Be accurate in the measurements ; here is your blue-print." Then he left me.

There I stood between the two face-plates of a wonderful machine and all the eyes of the men around glued on me, in charge of a costly lathe, trust and confidence placed in me ! With my mind made up to do my best I measured my work and started the lathe. One after another the wheels slowly went round, and the shavings fell like nuts to the ground.

Oh ! like a prince upon his throne I stood with folded arms and surveyed all the smaller fry below ; this was better than hitting my hand. I walked from one side to the other ; the lathes were self-feeding, and did not require my attention much. Beneath my eyelashes I squinted round and met many an upward glance. My eyes twinkled in defiance. I tried to twirl those few hairs I had under my nose, but I felt ready to burst with joy as I met the smile of the foreman in the distance.

I had to put up with a bit of jealousy by stepping into such an elevated position, but coming from the south, being blunt, my dialect strange, and being the possessor of large hands, they shrugged their shoulders and simply called me the Barbarian.

All this was very beautiful while it lasted, but everything comes to an end in this world, and the best of friends must part. The sick man came back and I was shifted on to a lathe nick-named the Funeral Car, because no man lived long on her. That means, he either left, met with an accident, or got the sack.

Most dreary were the hours of the night-shift on this lathe which I had to serve, and this was generally the time that accidents happened. The engines stopped between 12 and 1 a.m.; the silence was like being in a church, men would curl themselves up and fall asleep by the side of their work; then when suddenly the engines started again, some woke up and some didn't. I have seen many of these sleepers twisted round the shafting, losing their limbs; and many crushed by the cogs of the wheels.

One poor fellow's screams I shall never forget; he was in charge of the largest planer in the shop. Not often was this tremendous tool used to its full length. However, that night it was. He had forgotten to switch her on to the loose pulley, I suppose, and stowed himself away in the recess of the brickwork made expressly to receive the end of the bed when the machine worked at its full length. Slowly, inch by inch, the machine went on her way, then a fearful, long-drawn scream vibrated through the air. We heard the reversing gear automatically send the " planer " back, then the engines stopped and all was still again.

We all knew what had happened and went to
look for our mate ; we pulled him out, stood him
on his legs. He gave but one gasp, dropped
his head and doubled up like the shutting up of a
pocket knife. He was dead.

It was awful to stand at your lathe and pretend
to be at work, watching and waiting for the day
to break. Monotonous work, bad pay, long hours,
dangerous conditions, no comfort at my lodgings,
no sport or recreation, filthy streets, bad air—what
else was there for a fellow to do but to seek solace
in drink ?

Often on entering my lodgings have I grasped
for the bottle of Korn, which stood ever ready,
and let that slow-killing poison gurgle down my
throat to counteract the filthy stench that met
me on entering.

We were paid once a fortnight ; and on that
day it was as if the gates of Hell were thrown
open and ten thousand devils let loose. I doubt
whether there was one good man or woman in the
whole district surrounding Grabo or Bredo. To
me these villages will always remain Sodom and
Gomorrah, for it seemed that the Devil had it all
his own way.

Our week's work ended at six o'clock on a
Saturday. After paying the duns that waited
outside the gate, I usually went home and paid my
landlady ; then two or three chums would call,
and together we would go to Stettin and spend
our money in as many hours as it took days to get.

It was not so much the going ; I was often filled with the best of intentions. It was the coming home at night that made it so tempting to a young fellow ; the many dancing saloons and gambling dens at Grabo were a mighty fascination.

The ice and the snow had gone away, spring was at hand, and another pay-day had come. I was going from one saloon to another. Oh! those harpies knew so well how to play with a silly, giddy young fellow. I was made drunk, maybe drugged, I didn't know whether I was on my head or my feet. I was followed by three bullies, knocked down, and my pockets rifled of everything I had. Not satisfied with this, I was kicked and my pockets filled in a most disgusting manner. " For luck," they said, as they left me.

I was quite sober by now and wide awake, but as helpless as a child. I was covered in blood from many a wound, but none hurt me so much as the one inside : the agony of being treated in such a scandalous manner, the pain of shame. I longed for the very ground I was lying on to open and swallow me up.

Passers by helped me to my feet, and a mob collected. They asked me whether I was hurt ; I said " No," and shambled off to my lodgings. There was my landlady drunk on the floor, my mate snoring beside her, and the landlord with his boots on was in my bed. I stripped, washed and patched up my head, and put on clean clothes ; I sat down for a while and buried my head in my hands ; my thoughts went out to my parents, so far away, and a shudder went through the marrow of my bones, and I burst into tears. Through them I looked up to my knapsack on the wall. Mechanically I packed up what few things I had and walked out into the night, saying good-bye to no one.

Aimlessly I walked about, as if in a trance, with my head bent.

CHAPTER III.

In Thieves' Company.

FOR weeks I tramped through snow and rain, and at last found myself begging; the days were bad enough, but the nights were bitterly cold. My greatest anxiety was to get enough together to pay for a night's lodging; and so, one evening, I arrived at an inn, where many vagabonds, all sorts of professional beggars, men and women, organ grinders and thieves, sat round the tables, drinking and exchanging experiences. They looked up as I walked in, but said nothing, for who was I—only a tramp! One of that company died in the night. Jack Frost was in the air and nipped him.

On awakening in the morning, I saw, in the straw next to me, stripped of every garment, cold and stiff, an old man. His body was one mass of wounds and scars, his bald head a mass of blue and green bruises, his bones almost protruding through the skin, like a newly-fledged sparrow, only uglier.

I jumped up and ran into the arms of the landlord, who offered me a good breakfast if I would help him lift the body into a cart ; but I made an excuse and disappeared.

It is the easiest thing in the world to get into bad company, but sometimes nothing less than a miracle can get a fellow out of it. I had left the inn far behind, and was out on the open road, when I heard some one holloaing and shouting, and on looking round saw two of the guests of the night before hurrying up after me. One was a released convict, the other looked like a thief. They said they were going my way, and we might as well go together.

Germany has a novel way of dealing with its released prisoners : they dress them up in a suit of clothes made out of a sack, give them a march-route which they must produce and get stamped at every police station they pass, till they get to their native birth-place. If they deviate from the route laid down in their papers, they are at once arrested and sent home with a gendarme, and their native place has to pay the expenses.

Now this gentleman in the suit of canvas came from Dantzig, and had been many walks on the road ; he was as slippery as an eel, and with his straw hat cocked on one side of his head, as jokey as a Piccadilly swell. He began to address me in his prison slang, and remarked I was rather green. He asked me what religion I belonged to and said " I was a mechanic."

It was a strange experience, walking along by the side of real live thieves and listening to their talk. I tried several times to give them the slip, but it was no good, they found me out every time and hugged me, saying, " We will not let thee go." They were excellent cadgers, and overloaded me with kindness. For many days I was in their company and had to carry the bread basket.

I have never in all my travels met dogs in harness except in this part of the world : six, eight and ten large dogs, in splendid condition, pulling heavy carts along the roads. We sold the bread we had gathered to the drivers, and they fed their dogs with it.

I used to call on the trade pretty freely. Wherever there was a locksmith or a smithy, I walked in and took off my hat ; it wasn't work I wanted, for there was something mightily at work within me driving me away from it. It was the collection of the mates in the shop I was after to help a fellow on the road.

I once had the misfortune to walk into a shop where a fitter was wanted, but I told them I was a turner. At another shop they wanted a turner, but there I was a fitter. Yet at another shop they wanted both, and I stammered out that I could only work at the forge.

The weather was getting very fine now, all the trees were in leaf and new life seemed springing up everywhere, and so we entered one day a little village, surrounded by a dense forest. It was one of those quiet, beautiful, secluded little spots that seem as if they were cut off from the outer world altogether. The miller stood outside his gate, looking up the street ; at the smithy the fire had ceased roaring ; the church bells were ringing, and children with babies in their arms were gathered outside the porch. All the grown-ups of this little village must have been inside the church, for all the doors of the houses stood open, and no one was about. A wedding was being celebrated ; we caught a glimpse of the bride as we walked by, and when we had almost reached the last house in the village, the gentleman in the suit made out of a sack bethought himself of the fact that we had actually walked by all the houses and never asked anyone for a crust of bread. Without any further notice, he walked straight into a house. In a few moments he returned, holding a large square baking-dish, filled up with steaming meat, in his hands.

"Hurry up—run!" he said. We did, as fast as our legs would carry us, and were soon hidden amongst the trees. I felt strangely ashamed, guilty as a thief, and as we sat down on the ground to the feast, I tried to eat the bread I had steeped in the gravy, but it kept turning round and round in my mouth and seemed to choke me. I thought of the poor people who had lost their meat.

My two companions were not long in finding out what was the matter. Tearing the meat with their teeth like dogs, and the grease running down their cheeks, they nudged one another, and grunted " He is showing the white feather, he had better take the empty tin back to the house, and then go home to his mother."

I was in an awful condition; I could feel the blood running up to my head, but my limbs were numb and useless, my speech had gone altogether. Then all of a sudden something happened. A most hideous laugh burst upon our ears, and before us stood a great six footer: a man that looked somewhat like a tramp and yet he didn't, a heavy leather belt round his waist and long boots half way up his legs, fiery whiskers and in need of a shave. Rough and awkward as he appeared, there was something commanding about him, something fascinating in the look of his eyes, though he made them flash like daggers.

" That's it, my lads," he said ; " you are on the right track. You are sure to get into my hands at the finish." Up went his boot, and he kicked the one in sackcloth in the ribs and told him to clear out. Like a dog, on hands and knees, he did ; the other followed.

CHAPTER IV.

A Strange Comrade.

I SAT as if paralysed, unable to move; while he stood with his great arms folded, his eyes piercing my very soul.

"Which road are you going?" he said, in a tender voice.

"South," I murmured.

"Then come along, I'm going that way too. You had better get out of this neighbourhood quick," and he reminded me of an old saying, "Mitzegangen, Mitzepangen, Mitzehangen."

Oh! that I could explain the feelings of tender love that went all over me as he stretched out his hand and raised me from the ground. Hand in hand we walked together; I was loth to let him go. He asked me a few simple questions, and I somehow opened my whole heart to him and told him all my trouble. He listened patiently, made no remarks. Only now and again he stood still, put his great hands on my shoulders, and looked me fair and square in the face.

Oh ! those beautiful eyes ; who was he ? it seemed as if we had known one another for years. He told me about the company he had found me in : that those fellows were being searched for all over the country, that posters were outside every police station giving their description, that they had committed a most diabolical crime, and that whoever was found in their company would be branded for the rest of his life. A look up and a squeeze of his hand was all I could do by way of thanks.

The most wonderful thing that appeared to me then was that though my companion was big and rough and clumsy he was learned, refined, and as tender as a child. He knew every inch of the ground we were on. He took me through some lovely pathways, short cuts as he called them— away from the dusty highroads, where the perfume of new life was in the air and birds sang lovely. Now and again he would stoop and pick a blade of grass or a few leaves from the wayside, and tell me the use and names of different herbs. Again, in the forest he would tell me the age of the different trees, he would mock and call the birds, he knew their habits ; while for every star in the firmament he had something to say. He sang about poor wandering men until the tears streamed down my face.

At last we came to an inn. As soon as we entered, most of the guests finished their drinks and vanished. The landlord, hat in hand, addressed him like a gentleman.

We walked on in God's beautiful sunshine, singing like double-breasted goldfinches, and nature all so quiet seemed to be listening. He told me some wonderful tales that awakened thoughts of my childhood. Then for hours he would keep silent and still; now and again his beautiful eyes would meet mine, and a sigh would escape his lips, just as if he had a secret he dared not tell. Through every village we went the people knew him, and kept a respectful distance.

The dogs even, my greatest enemies, had a sniff and ran away. Women would throw up their hands in horror, snatch up their children out of the gutter and hide behind their doors; others would stand back as far as they could to the wall, and cross themselves as if they had seen the very devil pass by. But my friend, with his head erect, took no notice—didn't even smile.

Almost at the end of the village, he knocked at the door of a cottage and asked politely for a drink of water. The woman, with a hateful look on her face, brought a jug of water, put it on the ground, and stood back as far as she could get. He drank and thanked her, and I noticed the woman get hold of that jug with her thumb and finger, as if it was some poisonous reptile, and throw it into the middle of the road.

This all made me feel very strange, but I loved the man, for all that, more and more. He would not speak to me about his business—

only this much, that in the height of summer he had to look after mad dogs, sometimes slaughter a horse that had glanders, and bury cows with the rinderpest. " They called him the *scharfrichter*."

After three days in this man's company, he broke the news to me that we must part, and sooner than I expected. Just before we entered a good-sized town he stood still outside a house built up against a sandpit. A few spare poplar trees threw their shadow over it. Sunshine was all round, but his home didn't seem to get any of it. The place conveyed to me the thought that it was haunted—an evil smell, dogs barking, the intense loneliness, and a deep ditch added to this. He took down from the gate a long, wooden bar, and on opening the gate a rough dog flew out, jumped out at him and licked him. His joy was so great that I thought he would bite lumps out of him. They hugged one another, and over and over they rolled together.

On looking into the yard I saw heaps of bones in one corner ; in another, skins thrown down anyhow, tubs full of gore and fat and puddles that looked like congealed blood. I was mightily anxious to get away, and I told my friend I was in a hurry, so he shook hands and said he had been glad of my company.

I walked a little way, then sat down by the side of a brook, my thoughts going back to him I had left ; who was he ? Undoubtedly he was my friend, and showed love in every action, yet by every one else he was despised, hated and kept at a distance ; but he had delivered me from unspeakable shame. Without his help I should never have been able to have held up my head again ! He was the hangman of the county I was in.

CHAPTER V.

The Life of a Tramp.

ON I plodded through the town, meeting cold looks and sneers, longing to get into the country again ; busy people have no time for cheers.

The moon was out, one or two stars were twinkling. I wondered where I should rest, when I saw a light through the kink of a shutter. I knocked timidly at the door, and a voice said " come in." There sat the farmer in his shirt sleeves at the head of the table, ladling out the soup. Next to him sat his sons and daughters. Then the head servants, all in rank and file like the organ pipes, down to the little girl that looked after the geese and chicks.

The old mother who had so kindly asked me to come in beckoned me to a vacant chair, and put a plate of meat in front of me and a chunk of bread. Nothing was spoken, nobody stared, and I had a most comfortable meal. When finished, the master and servants alike kneeled down and in silence offered up prayer. Then all except the farmer and me disappeared.

" Leave your bag down here," the farmer said.
" Have you got any matches ?   I'll take care of
them, for there must be no smoking up there,"
and so he pointed up a ladder that went from the
room into the hay-loft, adding, " You can sleep
up there."

Oh ! it was lovely, a spring mattress indeed !
I sank in the hay up to my knees and soon I fell
fast asleep.   I was dreaming, and some time in the
night, in my dream, I fancied that the police were
after me, firing guns and rockets and pistols ; I
awoke, and true enough there was a cracking and
hissing, bang, bang and fizzing as if all the guns
on the 5th of November were going off together.

My heart seemed to stand still.   I groped about
in fearful darkness ; couldn't find the door I
entered by, didn't know which way to turn, until a
long streak of red, about half-an-inch wide,
appeared on the wall.   I went for it, and found this
was the door, and that it had a crack all the way
down.   I was looking through this at a house on
fire opposite.   With trembling hands I searched
for the bolts, pulled away the hay, and succeeded
in opening the door. What a sight ! A house
on fire from top to bottom, a huge mass of flames
starting straight up, no smoke, no wind, no
shouting, no water, no engine ; the cracking,
splinting and roaring of the flames was intensified
by the great stillness all around.

Fascinated, I stood for a moment ; then I
jumped for joy, and shouted and danced like

a lunatic. I felt almost drawn to touch the fire, it was so near ; then the roof fell in, and nothing but a great heap of smouldering embers left. I don't know how long I stood watching this, but I felt that ten horses could not have dragged me away. I was almost scorched.

Day was breaking. I looked round and saw a dozen white faces looking up at me from the street, and I thought it was time to get away, so slowly I climbed down the ladder into the room below. A pleasant smell of coffee was in the air ; the room was full of people, all looking at me.

I tried to catch the farmer's eye for my bag and matches, but he was just the only one that looked the other way, so I edged towards the door. I couldn't stand those earnest looks, that wonderful silence and shedding of tears. Then with a scream the old lady who had welcomed me in the night before ran after me, and with uplifted hands entreated me to partake of cake and coffee. As if in a dream I followed her, and she sat me down in the farmer's arm chair. I was as stiff as a log of wood, when she fell down and buried her dear old grey head in my knees, laughing, crying, praying, singing, all at the same time. Again and again she said " God bless you." " I could tell by your knock at the door last night that all was well." " Oh ! " she said, " didn't I tell you ? " looking at the others for confirmation. " Didn't I know something dreadful was going to happen this many a week, and if it hadn't been for my prayers where would you all be now?" "Yes," she continued, and kissing my hand, "we saw your wings and your outstretched hands warding the fire off. Now come and have some coffee."

The poor people who had lost their home were all gathered in that room. The women stared at me with big eyes, but a little boy came up and touched my sleeve to make sure I was alive and not a spirit. I was very quiet, I couldn't eat; they all shook hands—a dear little fellow kissed me.

It was only outside that I opened my lungs wide and found my strength again. I picked a flower, stuck it in my hat and strutted away, as rich as Baron Rothschild, finding myself, like the farmer's wife, laughing and crying at the same time. I couldn't feel any wings on my back, but maybe an angel stood by the side of me for all that.

Along I went for many a day, through forests, along rivers, over the hills, through valleys, jubilant most of the way. Sometimes the sun shone, sometimes it rained. Sometimes I met a friend, sometimes I was alone again. I was getting so experienced in human nature that I could tell a good man by the shadow he threw on the ground, and as soon as I caught sight of the crockery hanging in a room, I knew the woman.

Chapter VI.

Sturdy Rogues.

I HAD now walked right through one part of Germany, and was entering another.

I chummed up with two men, one was a butcher, one a tailor. It was good, for what one didn't know the other did. For miles we walked through tobacco fields. In the villages natives made "Havana" cigars! We bought them three for a penny. Then we passed miles and miles of beetroot; lump sugar was turned out of this. Then again we came to plantations of chicory, and wonder upon wonder, coffee was brewed from this. About the cheese I will not speak—people kept this in boxes outside their houses. But what took our attention was this: blue tablets greeted us on every door, saying "Begging is strictly prohibited here," and for further information the address of the Charity Organisation was given, with a warning that any-one caught giving would be prosecuted.

The police officers were dressed up as if they had come out of a pantomime, but were rather polite. "Gentlemen," said one to us, "would you kindly allow me to inspect your passports ? I am sorry to put you to any inconvenience, but we like to know who the visitors are that come to our country " ; and when he found our papers all right, he directed us to the office of that wonderful Charity Organisation, which was next door to the jail. We received, on producing our papers, about three half-pence each and good advice.

Hey! didn't we feel wicked after this. " Fancy," said the butcher, " three half-pence to keep us in grub till the next town is reached ! "

We noticed that the policeman who first addressed us was lame, and that some of the shopkeepers smiled at us, so we arranged that the butcher and I should each stand at the corner of the street, and the tailor run the gauntlet. It worked like a charm ; the harvest was great. Several times when " Hoppy " came in sight we dodged round the corner and opened new ground, but, alas, we did it once too often, and were caught in the arms of a gendarme. Breathless the lame policeman came up—all his politeness gone.

" You vagabonds ! " he said. " You have kept me over an hour from having my dinner ! Now then, off to the cosart ! "

The magistrate evidently had not much to do. He looked like a jolly young student, who was just disturbed smoking his pipe ; he tried to look fierce at us, but he couldn't ; he severely cross-questioned us, then sent the policeman out of the room, asked us how long we had been on the road, and how it was we couldn't get a job.   He gave us advice and begged us to abide by the law if we could.   " Take this," he said, and gave us a small coin.   Then he sounded his bell, and in came the gendarmes and the policeman.   " I sentence these three prisoners," he said, in a stern voice, " to be taken from here and marched out of the town, each by a different gate—east, north and·south.

An hour afterwards we were sitting in a ditch sharing the spoil, and watching ringlets curling from our cigars.   We spent the best part of the afternoon in this place.   The tailor mended our clothes while we washed the linen and spread it out on the grass to dry.   We soled our boots with a pack of cards, and brushed our clothes with the leaves of a tree.   We made arrangements for a glorious supper, and gentlemen we would be ; so when evening came we entered a village inn, and ordered a basin full of potatoes boiled in their jackets and a salt herring for each.

It may be interesting to know that all these salt herrings come from our shores, and are of the utmost value to Germany.   Little does the reader think, when he stands watching the lasses packing them in barrels at Lowestoft and Yarmouth, that millions of families live on them because they cannot afford to buy meat.   In that great country of Protection, the herring walks in duty free, and is eaten just as it comes from the pickle.

We slept in a bed that night. Next day the butcher got a job and the tailor disappeared.

For weeks I tramped about without a chum, and was getting very down-hearted indeed ; this hard and fast, merciless coldness of lazy bounders (kept by charity) doling out coppers to a beggar, behaving unseemly, saying things that hurt like the thrust of a dagger, almost drove me mad. What a difference it makes to give with a loving hand instead of a sneer ! But there, I was only a tramp !

CHAPTER VII.

A Cup of Cold Water.

AGAIN I stepped over the border and came amongst people of a different creed.

The sun had tanned my skin like leather—my hair had grown long, my clothes were held together with bits of wire and string, my feet were full of blisters. I was dying with thirst, and hadn't the courage to ask even for a drop of water. In the distance I saw the spire of a tiny steeple, and faintly I heard the sound of bells,—sometimes far away, sometimes near—in the stillness of the evening.

I heard them say: "Write to your father, speak of your condition." "No!" went back the echo from my heart. "Ten thousand times, No. I'd sooner die." Then, again, they would peal as if welcoming the weary wanderer home. I'd listen in rapture for a moment, then once again back went the echo "Not for me; not for me. I am forgotten, forsaken; nobody cares for me."

I passed a man, a woman and a child, with their heads bowed down, lisping their " Ave Marias " while the vesper bells were tolling.

I entered the long, narrow street of the village. Seats were outside the houses, the people were drinking in the dew of the evening, resting from their labours. The houses stood a little way up on a bank; my head was on a level with their feet. It was as quiet as in a church. I was the only figure moving; all eyes were centred on me. I heard the lisp of an old lady, "Some poor mother's son." I saw a giant six-footer, with arms like bars of iron, press a tiny little baby nearer to his heart, as if asking God to protect his child from ever becoming such a heap of misery as was going by. The bells were still ringing, "but not for me; nobody cared for me!" An old mother with her chin almost touching her nose, and with eyes like burning coals in her head, threw up her hands as if soliciting mercy. Little children grasped their mothers' aprons and hid their faces.

On I went, until half-way down the street, in the middle of the road, I saw a fountain—one of those homemade sort of affairs, a tree cut in half and the bark ripped off; just stuck in the ground anyhow, with a bit of quarter-inch gas barrel, and the water running out of this into a trough, made out of a tree also, but bigger.

There, at last, was what I had been longing for for hours—my tongue almost stuck to the roof of my mouth. Lo! what was the matter with me? helplessly I looked round; why didn't I scoop up the cooling drink with my hat, as I had done so often before? Why didn't I put my head in the trough and lap the water up like a dog ? No, I sank down on a stump and buried my head in my hands and cried like a child, and the bells rang softly all the time, " Not for me ; not for me."

I heard the latch of a door click. I didn't look up. " Nobody cared for me." My head rocked from one side to the other. " No, not a bit of it."

I heard somebody coming along ; I saw through my fingers the feet of a girl and a cup hanging from her hand ; I heard the sound of water bubbling into the cup ; I knew when it was half full ; I could tell when it was three-quarters full ; I knew when it was overflowing. Still the bells kept chiming " Nobody cares for me." And as if choking that lie back, the cup was thrust beneath my face, and I heard a voice say " Drink." Three times the cup was filled. I felt I could drink until the end. What was it I wanted so much ? Was it the water indeed ?

I walked away as strong as a lion ; I was the happiest man in the world, though I hadn't a shirt on my back ; I would not have changed with a prince. " What a treat," I said, " to be alive,"— and the vesper bells were still.

Every day brought its change,—sometimes I felt nearer home, sometimes further away ; sometimes I was in touch with the children of God, sometimes with the apostles of Hell.

CHAPTER VIII.

The Monk.

THE keen air and the icy wind up in the highlands made me feel as ravenous as a wolf. I could eat all day long. The worst times were the early hours in the morning. " No breakfast ! " Walk, walk, walk, with an empty stomach, to keep the blood in circulation,—pulling at my belt till I felt as thin as a wasp, fit to drop in half. When at these times I came across a Good Samaritan, a kind waggoner or road-mender, and received a few crumbs of tobacco, I would huddle my treasure, and shelter behind a tree, and drink in the aroma of the weed, which was food, comfort and warmth to me.

I passed a little cottage, which stood all by itself on the road. I knocked, and with my hat in my hand I stood, the wind ruffling my hair, when an old lady opened the door. I hadn't the courage to say anything. She knew, and didn't waste any time in asking questions. She shook her head, in fact she was so old, she couldn't keep it still, she clasped her bony hands, her look was full of sympathy.

" I would if I could," she mumbled, " but I ain't got a crust of bread. I'm hard up myself."

She hadn't got anything ! How strange, and yet my heart was going up and down like a concertina ; she gave me more than food, and I turned to hide a tear.

With " I forgot," she ran after me and put her old trembling hand on my shoulder, with the other pointing up the road she said, " Cheer up, you are just in time, you can't see it from here, but there is a monastery a little way round the bend and ever such a good father lives there. God bless you ! Make haste ! Goodbye ! "

O hope—wonderful charm—how soon it dries the tears ; my feet never seemed to touch the ground. A rainbow appeared, I walked on violets and roses. The earth heaved up, the sun burst out, the clouds disappeared, the wind laid down, and as I came to the bend in the road,—puffing and blowing, steaming with perspiration,—there, true enough, stood the monastery.

Instinct led me down towards the kitchen ; tramps don't enter the front door. On my left were the high massive walls of the building, on my right a row of trees with their boughs and branches touching the masonry, forming an arch over my head, blocking out the light of day.

Suddenly I came to a standstill : it was as if I had received a slap in the face. I stood, a great heap of palpitating, quivering misery. He, the greatest thief that ever lived ; he, who had followed me from my earliest childhood ; he, who had robbed me of all my money and my character, was mean enough to steal the hope I had received—rob a hungry tramp ! " No dinner for you to-day," he said.

Around the door of the monastery stood a crowd of leering men and women, who barred the way, making grimaces, shrugging their shoulders, pointing their thumbs. " Who are you ? What a cheek ! Go away ! "

Distinction and class—it reigned even among these professional beggars. I was just going to pick up my bundle—my red pocket-handkerchief that held all my earthly possessions—when the big doors of the monastery flew open.

If ever mortal has been permitted to get a glimpse of Heaven, it was then. Light flashed out in a stream. A well-kept gravel path was in the middle, as straight as an arrow, majestic trees each side formed an avenue, the leaves whispering, touching one another, blushing as they looked at me. I saw the tints of sage, some like myrtle, others glistened like emeralds, some white like silver, some brown, some red, whilst others turned crimson and had the lustre of beaten gold upon their face.

Far beyond and through the boughs, I saw the sky in its most delicate colours, blue and white and pink. Right in the centre of this living picture, of which the granite stones around the porch formed the frame, stood a monk. Love is the only word I can find to describe his face. He smiled upon the motley crowd below, had a nod and a wink for all of them. Oh! how my eyes were glued to the spot. " Would he look at me ? " " No," said a voice very close, and, as if to give the lie to this assertion, those lovely eyes beamed on me.

The crowd in the meantime huddled closer and closer together, begrudging me even a smile ; but the monk came down the steps, the crowd opened, formed a street, and he passed through the growling mob.

" To-day," he said, " the last shall be first." He drew me along, and banged the door in their faces. Hand in hand we walked that beautiful path—monks were going to and fro with sandals on their feet, reading their breviaries; not one looked up. In their silence I found their charity. The father who walked with me never asked me a single question. Had he said " Are you a Catholic ? " I would have responded with a string of " Ave Marias " and the whole " Litany." He knew I wasn't anything at all, and he didn't want to tempt me in the face of my misery.

We entered a large hall. I stood paralysed, not daring to go another step,—a long table was spread with the whitest of tablecloths, crystal glasses, china plates, silver spoons, knives and forks, glittering decanters, golden salt cellars, baskets of fruit and flowers, and tiny loaves of white bread, were arranged in the most lovely manner ; but the crowning effect of this glorious picture was a ray of sunshine that had found its way through one of the stained glass windows, and in it were hundreds of thousands of little sunbeams dancing about on the table.

" Sit down," said my friend. Helpless, I looked round. How dared I get near that table, unclean as I was. A door opened, a monk from the kitchen came in, carrying a huge plate covered with a silver cover. He put it down on the table where I stood. Another monk came and filled a glass of sparkling wine, and between them they took my bundle and stick out of my hands, squeezed me into a chair and carried me to the feast.

All this time my friend the monk stood at the head of the table with his hands folded, asking grace, like a Quaker, making no sound at all. Then he lifted the cover, and helped me, and said " Eat." The sensation of sitting at that table, and all those good things spread out before my eyes, the abundance of white bread and the clean tablecloth, the flowers and fruit within my reach ; to understand the sensation one must arrange to become a tramp. I had my fill ; it was good, but to this day I don't know what it was, for I couldn't see, the tears were dropping in my plate all the while.

This part of the world was nothing short of a paradise for tramps. No sooner was I out of one village than I spied another; for bacon and cider were handed to me almost everywhere, and the monasteries, which were dotted in the most lovely spots all over the country, I would take notice of and say " Where shall I dine to-morrow ? "

CHAPTER IX.

Austria—A Rough Reception.

IN time I arrived at Statt Steger. I went through the works, from one department to the other. In vain I implored the foremen to give me a trial.

" What a cheek," said one ; " look what you are. There are many respectable mechanics I could lay my hands on, but trade is bad."

" There is no opening here," said another. " Who do you think would work beside you, a tramp ? "

Like a double-edged sword, these words went to my heart, and with all hope abandoned I went on the weary march again,—climbing up and down hill, for many a week, towards Vienna, the wind blowing through my very garments and my feet again full of blisters, every part of my body sore. Hardly a living soul I met on the road now. The whole day I was often alone with my thoughts ; the silence at times was painful, and a fearful dread came over me. Even if a rabbit rushed across the road, I trembled.

One evening I heard far in the distance the yelping and barking of dogs. This brought me

to a standstill and I listened. The noise came
nearer and nearer as if on wings, and more hideous
moment by moment; swearing and screaming
of men and women as well as the snarling of
dogs on my right, on my left, and in front; I was
hemmed in.   Hell itself was let loose against
me,—trained mongrels threw me to the ground,
with bloodshot eyes and evil breath they dug
their teeth into me, rough hands pulled me to my
feet again and almost shook the life I had left out
of me.   Drunken yokels grinned and probed me
with spikes on the end of sticks, and laughed like
the very devil.   Oh! but all this was nothing
compared with the sight that met my eyes, and the
groans and shrieks that pierced my ears; about
twenty wretched human beings had formed a
circle round me, kept at bay by the dogs rushing
round all the while.   Some were blind, halt and
lame, some were lepers, with their faces half eaten
away, others were doubled up, too feeble to stand,
shivering with old age, couldn't keep their
teethless gums from trembling, which was more
horrible than the gnashing of teeth; yet for all
that I saw sympathy in their eyes, for I had
almost been stripped naked, and was ready to die.

" Your papers," shouted a bully.

" Yes," I cried, and then I saw he couldn't read,
so he flung them back at me.

This is the way Austria carries out its " Raggia."
At certain times of the year,—the day is kept
secret from everybody,—the headquarters of police

issue orders to all the Burgomasters and Mayors of the hamlets and villages throughout the country, to scout the highroads and byways to bring to book every creature who has no home. This, then, is the time the little Mayor looks for, to show his robes and to impress the poor with his boundless importance, and the servants get drunk in their zeal and courage.

Never did a chain of galley-slaves endure more kicks and cuffs and curses than this string of helpless beings gliding along in the night. I happened to be in the rear; when we arrived at a large farmhouse most of the prisoners had entered, the yokels had gone in too to pitch their tales, the dogs had disappeared. I could see by the light through the window the arrangements and the sorting of the captives. Horror seized me. Like the wind I rushed round the corner of the street and ran as I never ran before. Almost exhausted with fright and fear, I fell on my knees before a woman pushing a wheelbarrow in a brick-kiln, my hands went up in supplication.

"Help me!" I cried, "I've done nothing wrong, the 'Raggia' is after me!"

Like magic acted that one word,—women threw down their heavy loads, lifted me up and carried me to a heap of warm cinders, laid me out like a corpse and hid me with their skirts; when the sniffing curs arrived, they threw brickbats at them and challenged to fight the men with knives. When all was still and quiet, one of the women brought a basin of milk and some white bread, and fed me like a child, while others with their gnarled hands plied the needle and mended my garments; while another bathed my swollen feet and plastered up my wounds. Another sat silent beside me, stroking my hair and wiping my tears. So they worked and watched and cared through the night,—shovelling coals upon the fires, pushing their heavy wheelbarrows, instilling new life into me.

When the day shift came, my friends took me by the hand and led me for a long time through the country lanes from the high-road, handed me a parcel of bread and butter. " Cheer up," they said, " don't trouble about those demons, they'll never catch you any more. Good-bye. Think of us when you're far away." The sun came out in all its warmth, the hoary frost had disappeared, every blade of grass held a bead that sparkled like a diamond, the earth gave up its scent, the glory of the sky reflected itself in the river, and along its banks walked a great big over-grown child, who had come out of great tribulation, feeling that a miracle had set him free. I sat through the night up against a hayrick, with an old sack over my feet; I felt rich and that the whole world was mine. " After all," I said, " What do men live by ? "

The moon was shedding its light all around and I began to speak. " Shine, shine, shine good moon, into my mother's bedroom window; say you are looking at her child, tell her that you followed him through Hamburg, Bremen, Stettin, Berlin, Leipzig and Dresden. Say that even when you had to hide your face and the clouds were darkest, dawn was already nigh. Good-night, old chap!"

I was up with the lark in the morning, and fell in with a miller and a wheelwright, two boon companions, who could sing like nightingales. We made up our minds to go to Regensburg and try to get a lift to Vienna.

So I gave Munich the cold shoulder, for I had almost made up my mind to throw myself at my father's feet, though I knew I should fail at the last minute.

The Bavarian is born with music in his soul, and almost every evening at the inn,—especially in the Oberland—the country folks gather to dance and sing to the zither, throwing their sweethearts high into the air, catching them in their hands, screaming for joy and gladness. We, the strangers, were always kindly received, and when these great burly giants, in their close-fitting knee breeches and buck-leather jackets, found that my chums could sing, why they sat as silent as mice with their hands on their knees, overloading us with their " kreuzers."

In time we arrived at Regensburg, a very busy town indeed. Our first inquiry was for the Danube, and to our delight we saw a raft being put together, or more explicitly, five or six rafts

being coupled into one huge affair by means of
chains and ropes.   A small hut, built in the middle
of the raft, was being loaded with sacks of salt.
For many hours we hurried in all directions to find
the captain.   At last a kindly soul pointed him
out to me.   With my hat in my hand, and with
a mighty bow, I introduced myself and told him
our desire.

" You don't look much like a sailor excepting
about your feet, but I don't mind having half-a-
dozen after your pattern.   You will have to work
hard for what I give you to eat.   I shall be off in
an hour."

I brought the good news to my chums.   The salt
hut was sealed down with lead tablets by officials
in uniform.   We were seven hands altogether,
tramps, captain and crew, three with long oars in
front of the raft and three behind.

The Danube at Regensburg is but a baby, but
there are so many bends and ins and outs that
it takes a good deal of navigating and a great
deal of strength to steer clear of the banks.   Midst
a lot of cheers and shouting and hat waving,
the ropes were gathered in and the raft began
to move.

Lovely was the scenery along the banks of the
winding river, and I felt proud and of great
importance, pulling with all my strength, helping
to steer that great mass of floating timber.

When at intervals the Isar and the Inn joined
the Danube, the water was like a seething whirl-

pool, and we got wet to the skin. In the evenings we tied our raft up and went to the nearest village to sleep. We gathered cabbages, turnips and potatoes from the fields, and cooked them on board, but our funds were getting low when we were nearing Passau,—the border town between Bavaria and Austria,—where our raft would be overhauled by the Excise officers for contraband, the seals of the salt chest broken, where our passports would be examined, and where we had to produce a certain amount of wealth before we were allowed to pass the border.

My chums were down-hearted and full of fear, but I sought the captain and poured my tale of woe into his ear, with the result that he handed me a double-gulden,—a large piece of silver like our 5s. piece,—with " Don't tell anyone I gave you this," he turned on his heel and I disappeared.

Out in the open, at a table against the blue and white painted barrier, sat the officers, with stern looks and waxed moustaches, scrutinising us through their eye-glasses, making us shiver.

I was the first to appear, after the raft was tied up.

" Your passport ? "

" Yes, sir, your papers are all right, now show what you have in the way of money."

This perhaps was the proudest moment of my life. Like a millionaire, with a smile of haughty disdain, I dived down into my pocket and brought up a handful of buttons and obsolete coppers, and that great glittering silver piece on top.

" Pass on," said the officer ; but before I passed on that double-gulden had passed behind my back into the hands of the wheelwright.

He went through the same performance, but the poor old miller almost fainted when the officer jumped up in surprise at seeing so much silver in the hands of tramps.

Austria has but copper, and paper notes—gold and silver is scarce. The captain, I thought, had gone mad when we arrived, spasms seemed to stretch his mouth from ear to ear, his eyes were like a couple of beads, he threw himself down on the raft and kicked with his feet.

" Take 'em away," he shouted to his men, " or I'll die with laughing."

When we were afloat and he had recovered somewhat, I offered him his money back again, but the sight of it only drove him into another fit.

" Shut up," he screamed, " stow it," and he sent his arms flying like a windmill.

It appears that he too was anxious to pass the customs,—as he had something in a barrel underneath the raft,—but when he saw that they took no notice of him and paid all their attention to us, he wondered what it was all about, so strolled up to the scene, just arriving in time to see the passing of the silver coin, and then his pipe dropped from his mouth and he had to be led away in a most helpless condition. However, he got over it after we had passed the barrier, and we had a jolly fine time.

At Linz, about half-way between Regensburg and Vienna, I couldn't stand the damp atmosphere any longer ; my feet and nose had changed colour. I had also heard that at a town in the Oberland, called Statt Steger, work was to be had, so I asked the captain to let me off, and he presented me with a warm pair of socks and a pair of boots. My chums would not accept their share of the double-gulden. I had to keep the lot, and so I parted once more with my friends.

CHAPTER X.

The Snowstorm.

AUTUMN had now set in in earnest, and the wind was blowing cold. I knew nothing of the custom of the country, but the dialect of the people I understood, on the whole. The high roads were straight and broad,—never had I trod on better before,—the villages were neat and clean, and the type of inhabitants after my own style.

Many a strange customer I met on the road,— their language I could not understand, eagle-eyed, sharp-featured, pomade on their hair, dressed in sheepskin garments, and bandages round their legs ; they seemed to live on nothing else but *fat* bacon and black bread. The bacon they steeped in cayenne pepper and mostly ate it raw. Sometimes they would wrap a piece of newspaper round a chunk as large as my fist, put it on a skewer and light it with a match ; the whole thing burnt like tallow candle and the dripping they caught on bread. These Bohemians or Slavonians seemed to turn up everywhere, like the wandering Jew, and were quite harmless ; but with the vermin they carried it was not so.

I marched on with good cheer. I had resolved to take the first job that offered. Yes! I would turn over a new leaf, and with that purpose in mind I struck out for Statt Steger; a large gun factory was there. With the best part of the captain's gift in my pocket and well shod, I felt pretty free, and could face the gendarmes; I had no fear.

I wanted work now, but try how I would there was none to be had; so there was nothing for it but to go on the tramp once more.

The weather was getting very cold and tramps few. I went through Hungary, Pressburg, Komorn, Pesth, and so on. They are not pleasant recollections I have of this country; the villages were far apart, the roads bad, the language very difficult to master, and the people had not much to give away. My clothes and boots were in a dilapidated condition, and it was snowing; but that bitterly cold wind was worse than anything— as it blew across the Danube it went through my very bones.

I came to a miserable-looking village. I was starving, but had they offered me bread I could not have eaten it; my throat was almost closed up. I shambled along and, looking up, saw the name of the village on a finger post; that seemed the last straw, it was "Eland." What that means in the Hungarian language I don't know, but in German it means "misery."

I dragged myself to a tree that stood by the wayside. The country round was covered with snow, there was just a little place where no snow had fallen. I took off my knapsack, knelt on it and prayed to God to end my misery.

"O God," I said, "send me a bottle of brandy," and then I must have fainted. I must explain here that I was no drunkard then ; I became one long after this.

I knew, as everyone does, that if you go to sleep in the open in bitter weather you never wake up again ; but the pains of this terrible starvation would not let me sleep, they nearly drove me mad, and so I cried out to God to send me brandy. This was the first time I had prayed to God for nearly twenty years.

He answered that prayer ; a great comfort came over me, and I had visions of my father and mother, brothers and sisters. Then I remember no more until I felt an awful burning sensation in my throat, as if it were on fire, and I could hardly get my breath. I heard voices near me, but I could not open my eyes. At last they were pulled open by force, and I thought I saw an angel beside me, with such beautiful eyes, and holding my head so tenderly on his knee, trying to make me drink. It was only a "tramp," and my head was resting on the knees of another, and they had poured brandy down my throat. They told me it took a lot of rubbing to bring me to, and if it had not been for their brandy they would have failed. These two splendid fellows treated me like a brother. They wrapped me in a big coat, took me to an inn in the village, got some soup and took it in turns to feed me and comfort me. They accompanied me back into Vienna. This was the third time of going there. I found work the first day,—good work at Clayton and Shuttleworth's. I earned more money than I am taking now, and once more became a respectable member of society.

CHAPTER XI.

From Tramp to Inventor.

I HAVE now related my experiences as a tramp, and have given you glimpses of my early life. Now without any self-glorification, I am passing on to my life as an " Inventor," knowing the reader will not take offence at the high-sounding title adopted by a working man ; but for all that, I want you to look upon the " Inventor " as you would upon a butterfly just burst from its chrysalis, and remember the ugly caterpillar it once was, then you will see that it is possible even for a tramp to become an " Inventor." This world is full of transformation.

Cecil Rhodes once said : " The way to success is to get hold of an idea and stick to it." That certainly has been the case with many inventors, and has come true with me. " It's a long lane that has no turning." I have stuck to my idea for thirty-five years, and sticking is not all honey. You are often dragged over rough and stony roads, and are apt to slip at times ; but there are moments of comfort and rest that few people dream of, and when you seem weak that is just when you are strong. I have often sat in the midst of poverty, with tears of joy running down my face and my idea filling me with strength and song, and have been inspired beyond all expectation.

You will remember, I mentioned about a certain hangman in whose company I travelled for three days; I told you what a friend he was to me, and how I parted with him at his house. Also how I saw in his yard heaps of bones and congealed blood. By-the-bye, these were not from human beings; my friend was a horse-slaughterer as well, and in his spare time he boiled them down. I was curious enough to ask many questions about these evil-smelling things, and the outcome of that conversation was the birth of my idea—" Litholite."

In time, as you know, I came to Vienna and found work at Clayton and Shuttleworth's. My evenings were lonely, for I felt like a fish out of water; but my thoughts often travelled over the ground I had tramped, and dwelt at the house of my friend and his dry blood. I built great castles in the air. I saw tall chimney shafts. And so I brought home with me one night a jar of bullock's blood, sat up and dried it before the fire, and ground it in my landlady's coffee mill; out of an old candlestick I made a pair of dies, and with two square washers and a screw—a press. " Necessity is the mother of invention," and you never know what you can do till you try.

My idea was with me day and night. I hardly gave myself time for meals. I was astonished over the curious things this blood made (and so was the landlady over the smell). I used to sit and gloat for hours over a piece of black stuff, an inch square, and hide it at the least noise, fearing someone would come and snatch it away.

I was in the fever which all inventors, at one time or another, pass through. However, I got over that all right. In less than four weeks my beautiful samples, resembling jet and vulcanite, changed colour, the surface became rough, and the effluvia was unbearable. I had to leave my lodgings ; my landlady cleared me out. I gave way to despair, and sought comfort in public-houses.

A year or so after this I met my father in Berlin, and strange to say, he was inventing a machine to make buttons out of sawdust. I told him about my experiments with blood ; I shall never forget the inspired look that came into his face and the kind words he said. It came like a revelation to us both,—that sawdust needed a flux to bind it and blood a body to strengthen it,—so we mixed our ideas together, and some bi-chromate of potash to keep it all fresh, and the outcome of it was a patent and a large button factory in Berlin.

After this I was called to serve in the German Army ; but from there I soon deserted, and had to leave Germany all of a sudden and in a very great hurry, and came over here as a journeyman, obtaining a job in Cannon Street. From there I ultimately got to a job in Drury Lane, but how I got there I suppose I must tell.

I was then living in an underground room near King's Cross, out of work and hard up. Just then my boy made his first appearance in this world. I will not attempt to tell you of the intense joy, nor describe the fearful poverty I was in. Only this much, that my wife and girl were weeping and smiling, and there was nothing to eat in the place. I was dancing round like a lunatic with the boy, and the four of us were sleeping in one bed. Washing, living, cooking and sleeping down below on a level with the drains, and yet we were so happy.

" Cheer up," the mother said. " This boy is going to bring you luck ; I can see it the way his hair is parted." He was only a few hours old. Well, to make a long story short, he did.

That very day I picked up half-a-sovereign,—the only bit of money I ever found,—and we lived. Now a very strange thing happened ; while we were feasting on a tin of curried fowl and hugging that lucky boy, a rat-a-tat-tat came to the street door, and a gentleman came stumbling downstairs into our room and asked for me.

" Dear, dear," he said. " Is there any one in here ? Surely no one lives in. I can't see." And he put his hand up to shade his eyes, and his diamond very nearly knocked us down. He was a tremendous swell, so full of sympathy and so kind.

" Oh," he said, " I've found you at last," and then he saw that someone was sitting up in bed, and I am sure he wished to get out of it. " Well," he said, " you called on us a month ago and had some press tools for sale, have you still got them ? "

" Yes," I said, and pointed to them, like a millionaire.

" Oh," he said. " Will you bring them up to our works in Drury Lane ?   I am in a great hurry ; please bring them up at once. How much, £5 ? "

" Yes."

" Here is the money."

Now I ask you, didn't that boy bring me luck ? But that wasn't all. I delivered those tools, and had a long conversation with that gentleman in Drury Lane, and the outcome of it was a regular job at 50s. at week, and that is how I became foreman in a military ornament and helmet factory. I had charge of the press room and about twenty girls, all pieceworkers, and according to the ability of the foreman, it meant a good or bad Saturday to them. No words can picture the joy that came into our home. It wasn't long before I had a little house and a bit of garden at the back. And didn't we make a fuss of that boy ! The manager, who engaged me, was a very clever inventor and always full of ideas, and I had to work out some of his patents, and make a lot of automatic machines.   I had about two years there. One day he was showing some friends round, and among them was a foreign-looking gent, who pretended to be greatly interested in our machinery and made a great fuss over the ingenuity of our tools.   But it was all bogie; he hadn't come to see the works, he told me on the quiet, it was me he came to see, and I was just the man he wanted; would I come to Russia with him?

Well, the end of it all was that I gave notice to my employer, and started working for him at £7 a week; £70 was handed to me by the Russian Bank in Lombard Street to pay my passage, and so I started on my journey with wife and children.   Moscow was our destination.

CHAPTER XII.

Off to Russia.

WE took train to Hull, where I booked three berths on board the *Erato* to St. Petersburg. I gave my wife and children into the hands of the stewardess, and left them to get things a bit straight in the cabin; then in the company of the first and second engineers went ashore.

I remember standing on the quay and looking down on that beautiful sheet of water. It was a most glorious September afternoon, and I was so full of joy I longed to do somebody a bit of good, but didn't know exactly how or who, so I went with my companions from public-house to public-house and treated everybody that came along. I don't remember how I got back on board, but I know it was dark, very dark.

Next day was Sunday, and when the steward woke me my poor head was going up and down like a steam hammer, and I felt as if at sea. The steward helped me to dress and brought me a stimulant, led me up to the saloon for breakfast, and there I had to listen to an unpleasant lecture.

Everything was in a hurry and bustle : the gates of the dock stood open, so the passengers didn't take much notice of me, and the captain gave the signal for the engines to start ; then out we steamed into the North Sea.

Now when a fellow has been drunk, he generally gets up disagreeable, and with trembling and fear because he does not like to face the shameful things that come to his mind, and the only thing a drunkard does is to paralyse his brain ; that's what I did. I took Dutch courage and got drunk again. We were about a dozen passengers,—mostly ladies ; there was, however, a real gentleman on board, a Mr. Bombas, of London, and I believe by coming in contact with him, and through his kind talk and tactful ways, I was led to be a little better. Going on deck, I got a sly look from the engineer, and " How is your poor head, sir ? Will you have a look at the engines ? " I didn't want the engines, I wanted fresh air ; so I leant up against some timber, and tried to look very unconcerned and wise ; but I had the conceit knocked out of me, for the broken waves came over like buckets of water, and I got drenched to the skin,—still I stood my ground, and practised standing up straight on my legs.

We soon lost sight of all land, and for several days saw nothing but sea and sky, so I must tell something of our doings on board, and that brings me back to the ladies.

Dinner-time was the greatest feat of the day,— a splendid musical box was set to work in the saloon, and it was astonishing to me how good the food tasted with music, and how quickly it disappeared. The Captain was a man of great tact, and took all the ladies under his wing. I sat at the end of the table and so did Mr. Bombas. We got into conversation with our eyes by winking at one another, over those dressy, painted, artificial sort of ladies. There we sat opposite each other,—the rough, careless, uncultivated workman looking into the eyes of the refined gentleman,— and we understood one another so well without speaking a word.

After dinner the Captain used to come up to us and shake hands with Mr. Bombas, and with a look, solicit his sympathy and get it. Then he'd make a grab at my arm and drag me into his private study, push me into a chair and heave such a sigh, till I fairly began to roar ; I laughed until the tears trickled down my face,—it was all so comical, as good as a pantomime. Then he'd start growling like a thunderstorm, breaking away at a box of cigars and throwing a handful at me. " Take that," he said, " you unfeeling fool! " and out of a cloud of smoke came something very unparliamentary about ladies. " Give me a plain woman," he shouted. " I can't stand these painted and perfumed dolls, I shall be going mad, and yet, you see, it is my bounden duty to make a fuss of them; it's part of my day's work. If I don't, they will start writing letters to the company and I should get the sack."

The captain cooled down after a while, and said the worst of it was they weren't ladies at all. " Their fathers work at a mill and save up a lot of money, then the daughters get the fashion fever, change their dresses half-a-dozen times a day, and what with tight-lacing and elephant-ivory teeth, they must put on a little rouge just to keep up their complexions. But," he said, " I wouldn't mind all that, so much as the way they twist their mouths when they speak and smother themselves with scent." He then told me the genuine ladies that came that way were working men's wives.

Well, I sympathised with the Captain's wine and cigars, and went on deck, and that great ship would rock about like a cockle-shell, and the waves ran high as mountains; many a time the ship dipped down as if never to rise again. That's the time to make one feel what helpless creatures we are, and that's the time we plead.

We knocked about like this for several days, and we were nearing the Skager Rack; we passed Denmark and Sweden, and I could see right into Copenhagen. Very near to us rose a majestic palace,—a high and stately building with many glittering windows, and a

solemn atmosphere seemed to hang around it.
I think it was called " Hekingfoer." We had to
steam away very slowly and carefully—we could
almost touch land on either side—and by degrees
we got into the Baltic. The sea was like a looking-
glass, not a ripple to be seen. It took the Captain
all his time to bring life into our midst ; the
journey was getting monotonous, but one evening
we saw a peculiar light in the distance, and we
jumped to all manner of conclusions as to its origin ;
at last it dawned upon us that it could be nothing
else than a ship on fire, and so it was. It was an
awful sight. It was one of Bailey and Latham's
floating coffins, as the men called it,—a large iron
vessel, stacked up with wood like a timber yard,—
and was one mass of sparks and flames. We all
felt quiet and solemn as we looked up to our
Captain.

" Would he attempt to save life ? " Some of
us got the shivers when he told us that he dared
not go near it, for we had some inflammable stuff
on board. I believe a silent prayer went up from
every soul on board. How near it brings one to
God when death is staring you in the face !
For three hours we lingered around that burning
ship, but could not see any life. The Captain
said it was a blessing the sea was calm so that a
boat could live. We watched the fire burn down
to the water's edge ; it was a dreary sight, that
great floating iron skeleton, with its damaged
ribs and glaring portholes.

We were nearing Kronstadt now,—the strongest fortification in the world,—and we saw search-lights in the distance. Then as we drew nearer the signal came for us to stop, and half-a-dozen dirty, hungry-looking soldiers came on board and began sniffing round our luggage. It was just here I noticed a very disagreeable smell, and of course put it down at once to those soldiers, but the Captain said it was the smell of the land, and I would have to get used to it.

The engines started again, and we entered the "Neva"; it is hardly worth calling a river, it is only like a canal with stones piled up on either side. Shortly we beheld St. Petersburg looming up before us, with its palaces and golden cupolas glittering in the sun; we seemed to steam right into the middle of the town. We were surrounded by houses on all sides, and every window seemed to be filled with wagon-loads of monkeys,—hanging half-way out, in red shirts, glaring and jabbering and shouting; as for hair, well, I have never seen such mops or anything else like it.

The Captain took me on one side and gave me a few wrinkles about the Custom House officers and roubles, and as if by magic my goods were all passed; but one of the ladies had an awful bother. They turned everything inside out. How it's done! I thanked the Captain for all his kindness, shook hands all round, and then my troubles began. My passport was made out for me and family, the names of wife and children didn't appear on it, and that was against the law of Russia, so I had to fetch out more roubles to square it. It is wonderful how it is done!

Now I didn't understand a word of that horrid language, and when I asked for Moscow, no one had ever heard of such a place; but, somehow, after a lot of bad language, I managed to load all my belongings into three cabs, put my wife in one, the girl in another and I followed with the baby boy. Shall I ever forget that ride? The drivers standing up and lashing their horses, shouting and holloaing; the screams of my wife and children, the dust and stones in the road, and every moment I thought we were going to be pitched into the canal. It was shocking, and the more I expostulated with the drivers the more furious they drove. I wonder we ever got to the station alive. I wouldn't go through that ride again for a pension.

Now at the station, I thought we were all right, but the people thought I was mad; there wasn't any such place as Moscow, but they would give me a ticket to Mosqua. Anyhow, I chanced it; I didn't know whether that was right. After a lot of palaver I got on the right platform, giving out roubles right and left all the time.

Engines and carriages are after the American style, sort of Pulman cars, very comfortable, and you can step from one carriage to the other. I thought I was mesmerised when I opened the door of the nearest compartment, while my wife almost fell on her back. It was like a drawing room—

red velvet seats, and ladies sitting on the sofas smoking cigarettes. My wife pulled me back, but we were hustled into the next carriage, and that was just the same. Oh, dear! I had a nice time of it. My wife would insist on standing up in front of me. She didn't like those ladies' ways; but you see in Russia it is the custom for ladies to smoke.

The journey was through flat country, forests and swamps. Nothing picturesque there; we passed through a good-sized town called Tver, and in a day or two, if I remember rightly, we arrived in Moscow.

Moscow is unlike any town I have ever seen; very antique, very old and very clean, until you come into details, of course. They have no waterworks, no supply and no canalisation, and no sewers. The houses—some are built of logs and some of stone; the pavement is rough and hobbly; churches are all over the place, and bells are tinkling from morning till night in some parts of the town. There are magnificent modern buildings fitted up with all the latest improvements,—telephones, electric lights and lifts; it seems very strange to the mind, the ancient and the modern jumbled together. It is like walking through a fairy tale,—tram cars and monasteries, barracks and foundling hospitals, wooden shanties and Carrara marble palaces, west-end dandies and Tartars and Circassians, all in a heap.

The industries in Moscow are going ahead by leaps and bounds ; factories are constantly being erected, bossed over by French, American and English engineers. The country people flock to the town in their thousands. Wages are very low—pay-day once a month,—but the wants of the Russian workman are very few : a red shirt, a pair of long boots and a sheepskin coat is about all he needs. A bed he does not want, anywhere down on the floor will do for him ; he sleeps in his clothes, and never takes his boots off,—he might lose them. Besides, all his money, comb, knife and looking glass are stowed away in them. Water being scarce and dear, he does not use much for washing ; but he must have a bath once a week, his religion demands it. Tartars, Cossacks, Kalmuks, Armenians, Persians and Mushics are all tarred with the same brush, more or less, and make a rare show with their religion.

The ordinary Russian worker, with all his faults, isn't a bad sort of fellow : he is quick at grasping and understanding, he has a large, warm heart, and is easily moved by sympathy. He will do almost anything if he sees a glimmer of love ; but he is held in a powerful grip by the police and priest.

I will illustrate to you the simple, childlike confidence of the ordinary Mushic. I was living in a wooden hut near the Sparrow Hills, outside the town. It was Easter Eve. A knock came at my door and in stalked a great, awkward-looking fellow with his hat in his hand, bowing and saluting down to the ground, beating his chest and crossing himself, and calling upon his saint to bless me. As soon as I recognised who he was I got up to throw him out, but he dodged me, went down on his hands and knees, and embraced my legs and kissed my feet. I became furious, and kicked him from me. He quietly rose, brushed his long hair from out of his face, and stood silently looking at me, with tears trickling down his cheeks. I couldn't stand that, so I asked him in a gruff voice, what he wanted ?

" Oh, Mr. Hess," he said, crossing himself all the while, " I know I have wronged you. For the love of God forgive me ; in an hour it will be too late. Come with me to the Kremlin, I want to embrace you, I want to see Christ," and down he went wallop, kissing my feet again. I didn't kick him this time, but I didn't like it.

Now I wanted to see this affair in the Kremlin, so I told him it was all right, and put on my hat and coat and went with him.

The Kremlin is a magnificent block of palaces, churches and municipal buildings, and the river Mosqua runs along one side, and a high wall encloses the whole ; and many historic gates are there—one goes by the name of the " Holy Gate"—and a policeman is always on duty to see that you uncover your head ; no matter if it is thirty degrees below zero, your hat has got to come off.

From the Kremlin you have a splendid view over the town. It is a lovely sight, clear atmosphere, no smoke (for they haven't got any coal), the green painted roofs of the houses, and the river forming a horse shoe, in the distance the Sparrow Hills, where Napoleon stood with his mighty army. In the Kremlin is the church where the Czar has to attend several times a year, and in it the bell that is only sounded once a year. The Imperial residence is also close by, and opposite an immense jail, where all the convicts of Russia are collected, booked and numbered for Siberia. Cannons and heaps of shot are arranged as ornaments wherever there is a space,—they are the relics of Napoleon, when he left in such a hurry. On a high pedestal also stands that great historic lump of metal " The Holy Bell."

At some distance my companion and I turned into the high road ; all was still and dark, only a few stars twinkling overhead. There were many people moving about, but in their felt shoes and on the snow they couldn't be heard. As we went on the crowd grew larger, and, if possible, more silent,—it seemed as if it were a crowd of spirits fleeting along. At last the mob numbered hundreds of thousands, and just outside the Kremlin we came to a standstill ; the crowd was so packed, we couldn't get any further. All of a sudden a sound floated through the air, as if a great gun had been fired. It was the first stroke of the Holy Bell, and as if by magic light came into every place : thousands, millions of candles were lit in the crowd, in the churches, in the steeples. All the bells of that great city began chiming, and a mighty shout went up, " Christ is risen ! " The people rejoiced and embraced one another, enemies begged forgiveness, the rich kissed the poor, gave them tidings of good, shouting " Christ is risen ! " The poor peasant beside me put his arms round my neck and kissed me, and in blessing his enemy, saw Christ.

Such was the type of men over which I had charge, and the firm I went to Russia for, not being successful, and the old love of my invention still being as strong as ever within me, I fixed up a room like a doctor's shop, with pestle and mortars, bottles of acids and alkalis, and there paid my attention to marble, alabaster and limestone. Well, I thought I had found the philosopher's stone. I was in paradise, and all the riches of the world were mine, when the blow came. I built up a factory in Moscow, and got into the hands of a Russian Jew; but there—I needn't tell you how that ended. Again I sought comfort in drink, and came back to England penniless, and lived in Tottenham.

Chapter XIII.

Conclusion.

I DON'T know whether any of my readers have ever tasted the bitterness of going back to the bench after being a boss for many a year, but it is an awful pill to swallow, and it is only time that can take that bitter taste away; and it is very hard to a man that has learnt his trade and been a leader of hands to carry out the orders of a so-called foreman who pretends to know his work but doesn't. Such was my lot, and it goes without saying, I drifted into a state of utter carelessness, and got hold of things that dragged me down. God knows I was sinking, but, in the nick of time, the Adult School threw out the life-line and saved me.

I was then living in a turning from Farringdon Street, and at once I began to lay my money out differently. I bought a lathe in the cattle market and a vice at a stall, fixed myself up some benches with the aid of bacon boxes, and though I worked all day as a journeyman in Kentish Town, I worked ten times harder at home; I was sticking again

72

to my old idea. I wish I could explain the intense joy that came over me, and how I seemed to breathe in an altogether different atmosphere.

Now I was filled with strength and energy by the hand-shake I received on the Sunday morning. How it brought back all the remembrances of long ago, and reminded me of great love and friendship. About this time I dropped into Lyndhurst Hall, their first Exhibition, and it was a great inspiration to me. I met men who thought much the same as I did, and who had gone through hardships and troubles—some noble characters. I also saw how I had stood in my own light, by wasting my time in public-houses instead of using such places as the Institute at Lyndhurst Hall; and through a few tactful words from one of the lady teachers I gave up the drink, and by leaps and bounds my invention grew. I found out that I could do away with much unnecessary labour in shaping all sorts of goods, as well as a method of using up waste.

My material was then in the shape of dough, and I pressed it in heated dies, using it for inlays. I found a partner and built up a factory in Clerkenwell; I trusted him and didn't trouble about an agreement,—an old fault of mine,—and the same thing happened here as in Moscow: when I was pumped dry I was done with.

I met with an accident and was laid up for twenty-two weeks, and I thought I should never do another stroke of work again; but I was cared for : a friend came forward and offered to start me in business, and did. Now was the time to set to, and show what I could do, but almost at the first start I met with fearful difficulties. I bought a steam engine and boiler. The latter had been very badly used, and instead of turning out work, I had to go mending and patching, and walk about with my life in my hands, expecting every moment to go up in thin air.

After this trouble was over the drains in my workshop went wrong, and I had to go through weeks of trouble, disappointment and care ; then the rain and wind loosened the tiles on the roof of the building I was in, and almost flooded me out. In the midst of all these trials I had to produce goods for sale and also improve my material,—for it was not yet to everybody's liking ; some said it was too heavy and others found fault of various kinds.

All this was a training to teach me how to get over obstacles, though I couldn't see it at the time. Never before did I realise what manufacturing meant. Filing, turning and smithing is nothing, one has to wear cuffs and collars, and sometimes a frock coat on the top of all that, and go out to solicit orders ; and when other men go home to rest, the manufacturer sits down and does his correspondence and tries to balance his accounts, and in the morning when he wakes up he often finds he hasn't been asleep.

How often have I sat in the midst of despair, with all my hopes tumbling to pieces like a house built of cards. How often have I longed to be a tramp once more, to get rid of my anxiety and care. Yes! but what about my responsibility?

In one of my darkest and yet lightest hours I remembered that tree out in Hungary, where I cried to God for mercy,—the same thing has happened all over again. I realised once more that it needs neither church nor chapel to get deliverance out of trouble: that under that tree, or in a workshop, or in a bare room, one can hear the still small voice whispering words of comfort and cheer. Now I have set down facts just as they happened; the future is hidden in a shroud. None of us can look behind that curtain.

Whether the " Inventor " has to go on building up for others, or whether he will reap the fruits of his own labours, time alone can shew.

———

[Charles Hess died in the German Hospital, London, on the 15th of September, 1908, after a painful illness, borne with much fortitude. He kept up his interest in Adult School work to the very last, and had undertaken to address a large meeting in Wales to further the movement. A large company of comrades gathered at his funeral, which took place at the Friends' Burial-ground, Stoke Newington. At the simple service which followed many bore testimony to the influence of his life.]

ESSAYS.

What the Adult School has done for me, and how it did it.

HOW helpless I feel to express what the Adult School has done for me. I hardly know where to begin. My thoughts are all of a heap, racing one another, each one eager to be the first; but the thankfulness and joy in my heart can never be given in ink. The proof of the pudding is in the eating. What was I five years ago? Unclean! but now I am washed and fit to be seen.

In Stoke Newington the Shepherd found me, and a Quaker lady led me to Bunhill. I didn't want any Bible class! I had no will of my own. I didn't want a prayer meeting! All hope was gone. In the 5th of Luke, from verse 18, is a story very much like mine, only instead of men bringing me in, it was a woman, and when the Lord saw her faith my sins were forgiven me.

Shall I ever forget that first Sunday? Like a great child I sat, only more awkward. I didn't know where to put my legs and I didn't know what to do with my hands, and I couldn't hold my head up. I longed for the floor to open and let me down. I felt like a leper sitting among a lot of clean men. Fancy me sitting for the first time in my life listening to what Jesus said to Nicodemus, and the Bible in front of me. How I longed to get out of that door—I wasn't used to breathing such air.

Strange it seemed to me. There was no parson, no ceremony, and no one asked whether I was saved. Somebody said the School was for drunkards as well as teetotallers, and for those that didn't believe anything at all. That sort of talk did me an immense lot of good, and I felt comforted in a way I cannot explain. But for all that I wanted to get out into the street again.

I had almost reached the stairs when suddenly a hand was pressing mine, and the President, with a heavenly smile, said : " We thank you for your company, will you come again ? "

" Yes," I said, but didn't mean it.

All through that week I felt that grip ; wherever I went I saw those eyes. How could I stop away ? Sunday after Sunday I came.

What was that power drawing a rough chap like me ? Was it that hand-shake ? Was it the kind looks all round me, or was it the place so choke full of prayers ? The only answer I can find is in Luke xiii. 7-9, only instead of three years read forty-three.

How thankful I am that drink had not robbed me of all my brain. How glad that I still had gumption enough to understand it was my last chance. How happy and rich that I listened to the Spirit within.

My conduct changed; I became more select in my companions, refined in my talk, considerate to my wife, took more interest in my children's welfare, and began to feel a little respect for myself. I thought about my "wasted life," from the time I ran away from home. It seemed "Though I was a great way off my Father saw me and had compassion."

The spirit of Bunhill reminded me of many things. Deeds that had been buried in my heart for many years. Like the woman at the well of Samaria, I can truly say "He told me all I ever did."

For about two years I never missed a Sunday. I could manage to chime in with singing a hymn but could not bring myself to pray; I always got smothered with tears, and felt unworthy. It seems wonderful to tell, but friends again cared for me. I felt their prayers touch me before they went up to Heaven.

It wasn't exactly all honey at times. I had to take the bitter with the sweet. I had to pass under darkening clouds and walk through thorny paths, and had to put up with many a sneer; but I grew in strength and realised that I was being kept, and overcame these troubles, hard as they appeared. I was often touched by the testimony of simple men. How their experience tallied with mine !

The School became my birth-place. I knew what it is to be new-born. The Lord Himself taught me how to pray, made me free and independent. He is the best Friend I ever had. May the School grow in grace, and be a haven to many more shipwrecked outsiders. It is a sure anchorage to wasters like me.

February, 1900.

Why does an Adult School succeed?

"He who dwelleth in Love dwelleth in God, and God in him—God is love."

LET me say at once, because it carries out in practice what it teaches. To say " that a little knowledge is a dangerous thing " is to quote a proverb too often misapplied. Ignorance is far more dangerous than a little knowledge, practical and theoretical. A man possessed only of theoretical knowledge could no more explain what an Adult School is than fly,—even credit such a man with the best theological knowledge, and the knowledge of every text in the Bible.

The man with a practical knowledge is in a much better position, for he handles the work he is engaged in and grows capable of judging the love he receives. Far be it from me to say that theory is of no value, but if the possessor of theoretical knowledge cannot put it to use, what is his knowledge worth ? Theoretical knowledge and practical experience work hand in hand together. No man lives to himself in the Adult School ; if it were otherwise it would be a bad job for many a bright and happy life.

This essay must serve as a rough sketch to explain what words can never tell. Careless, thoughtless, illiterate men come into the School; they may lay hold of the offer the Adult School gives, or they may throw it away, but for all that, deep down in every man's heart is the desire to be good, to be a better man than he is. This treasure is the secret of the Adult School; it sparkles brightest in times of despair, its light flashes when night is darkest.

The Adult School is an old establishment, was started in a carpenter's shop at Nazareth; all sorts and ranks and conditions of men came to it. Creeds didn't trouble them much; they had lost faith in scribe and priest, couldn't stand their talk, nor swallow what they said.

In coming to the School of Christ they listened to a man, and found in Him a Friend; these were the Founders of our Adult School in England.

" Why does an Adult School succeed ? " Because it speaks in a language men can understand, and has but one platform, on which every scholar has a right to stand, be he minister, shoe-black or prince. God is no respecter of persons; it is character that tells.

The Adult School does not turn Christians out wholesale, nor ask any one whether he is saved. No sensible Adult School man would expect an apprentice to become a carpenter in a day, nor would he want to be stuffed up with a lie.

The simple truth of the life and work of Christ is taught; nothing shoddy, nothing second-hand; the doors are open to everybody. The desire to be a member is the only price one pays. Through this wasters are reclaimed, and men who never attended a place of worship realise that they are standing on holy ground. It does not matter how a man is dressed, whether he wears a frock coat, choker or high hat—it's not clothes, it's men the School seeks. The Adult School does not lift men into Heaven, but brings Heaven down into their lives.

Men have for ages yearned for an Institution like this, where they can meet together irrespective of caste and ceremony, puffed up pride and respectability; where they can reason together, get strength and sympathy, and equip themselves to fight life's battle. What would not other countries give for a privilege like this?

"A little help is worth a deal of pity," and herein lies the charm of the Adult School. The rich help the poor, the educated help the ignorant; if one member is in trouble, the whole School feels it; a current of wireless electricity moves each man to practise Christianity instead of words; bread is given, tears and sorrow are wiped away.

Had I the tongue of an angel and used one thousand five hundred words, I could not say one half as much as by pointing with my finger to the picture of the Good Samaritan; the Adult School succeeds because it lifts men up.

Thousands are down, robbed and wounded by the greatest thief that ever lived ; their money and manhood gone.

" When wilt Thou save the people ;
    Oh ! God of Mercy, when ? "

I wonder if the priest felt he was doing his duty when giving out a hymn. I wonder if the Levite got over his curiosity by the congregation singing to him. I wonder what prompted the Samaritan to care for the stranger ; did he owe him anything ?

The Religion of Life Series.

EDITED BY RUFUS M. JONES, M.A., D.LITT.

The purpose of this series is to present in small compass and convenient form some of the living thoughts of the Christian Mystics of all ages. Special attention will be given to the contributions of Quaker writers.

Many of the passages are noteworthy for the beauty of their thought and the reality of the faith they give evidence of.

The first two volumes will be ready in May. Others will follow at short intervals.

Cloth gilt .. .. **1/6** *net.*
Leather gilt .. **2/6** *net.*

Headley Bros., Bishopsgate St. Without, London, E.C.

A BROTHER OF MEN.

The Life of William White, of Birmingham.

Cloth Limp, 1/-,
Cloth Boards Gilt, 2/6 net,
post free.

London: Headley Bros.,
Bishopsgate Without, E.C.

www.ingramcontent.com/pod-product-compliance
Lightning Source LLC
LaVergne TN
LVHW081347060426
835508LV00017B/1464